C000157251

HOW TO SUPPORT A CRAP FOOTBALL TEAM

Steve Crancher

Illustrated by
Ash

Ian Henry Publications

ISBN 0 86025 542 5

Website: www.crapfootball.co.uk

Published by
Ian Henry Publications, Ltd.
20 Park Drive, Romford, Essex RM1 4LH
and printed by
4Edge Ltd., 7a Eldon Way, Hockley SS5 4AD

Preface

In January, 2004, I went to watch a Tuesday evening match along with approximately 3,000 other fools like myself. Together we braved sub-zero temperatures and watched disheartened and £15 the poorer as twenty-two lower division players kicked the ball around aimlessly. The match ended in a 0-0 draw.

As I left the stadium I turned to my friend and said, "Never again." But I knew I was kidding myself. Two days later I was queuing in the snow for tickets to go to the next away match in an unfashionable part of the country.

Those two days inspired this book.

SC

ACKNOWLEDGEMENTS

Thanks to
Greg Fidgeon, Steve Maltby,
Rob Mellett, Kerry Sheehan,
Marge, the Groovy Roovers,
Cliff, and Sid (my dad, who took
me to that first match and tried
in vain to make me support
Arsenal).

~ Introduction ~

Sadly, this is not a book full of optimism, enthusiasm, or joie de vivre.

It is not sanguine. It's the opposite, in fact. It is desolate, dismal, even bleak. And yet, having read it, you will continue in your pursuit of the impossible dream. It will merely confirm to you what you already know.

All that remains is whether or not you have learned to recognise that truth.

This is not a pastime for the loner. Defeat after defeat cannot be borne with no one to grumble with. Supporting the losers is a social activity.

You have to be determined and dogged. The fainthearted will fade away early on. Those of a weak constitution will be incapable of withstanding the never-ending incompetence. Mettle is a requisite.

If you're still reading, it's likely that you need help. You could try seeing the doctor. You could even try a visit to a psychiatrist.

If so, you need to be prepared. He will ask you difficult, soul-searching questions. This book will help you to understand exactly what you put up with.

You're about to find out how to support a crap football team.

~ How it all began ~

You're 8 years old. The world is full of good things - nice things, like sweets, hamburgers and pocket money that you can spend on anything you want. You're full of hope. Everything is just dandy!

You watch football on TV. You're wide-eyed at the silky skills, the mazy runs, the 30-yard curly free-kicks. The excitable commentator tells you how great it all is and you believe every word.

Your dad tells you there's a football team down the road who play in division three.
'Are they on the telly?' you ask.
'Sometimes,' he replies.
'Can we go and see them play, dad?'
You have sown the seeds of misery. You are expecting to be entertained. You are about to make a huge mistake…

The stadium makes a big impression on you. OK, so the stadiums on TV don't have trees, but at least it's got proper stands where people can see the pitch when they're behind other people.

And they've got a proper glossy programme in colour. And there's a place where you can buy hamburgers and chips. And the supporters are wearing scarves with the name of the team on them. And the grass… well, the grass is the greenest grass you've ever seen in your whole life. You'll never forget that first impression of just how brilliantly green it is.

And then everyone claps because the teams are running out onto the pitch, so you join in with the applause. Suddenly you feel part of the crowd and, as you clap, you smile up at your dad and he smiles down at you. You feel proud. You feel excited. You are full of anticipation.

'Which team is ours, dad?' you ask. It's a stupid question but one that has to be asked on that first visit.

Whatever the answer is - blues, reds, clarets, yellows, oranges, whites, greens, stripes, hoops - it sounds good. Sometimes they say the same on telly. Other teams wear the same strip, so this team must be like the other teams.

So then you look at the players, but something ain't right…

Some are fat,

    some are thin,

        some are very tall,

            some very little,

and the one with number 5 on his back looks quite scary.

Your dad tells you that the one with grey hair used to play in the premiership.

'Which team, dad?' you ask, excitedly.
'Tottenham,' he replies.
'Oh well,' you say. 'Never mind.'

The people around you are all the same but all different.

One shouts 'Come on you [nicknames]!'

Another says '4-0, that's what it's gonna be.'

Another says 'Oh no, that bloody Wiggins is playing. He's bloody useless, he is.'

Another says 'Three points today and we'll only be 7 points behind the play-offs.'

Some people seem happy. Others seem a bit angry. But still you're excited and full of anticipation.

Then the ref blows the whistle and starts the match.

Now the people around you are shouting out things you don't quite understand.

'For crying out loud, get to the byline.'

'That was never offside.'

'Come on linesman, keep up.'

And 'Whose side are you on, ref?'

On the telly, the commentator tells you everything, but he doesn't answer questions. So you ask your dad 'Is the ref on our side or their side?'

'I think he's on their side,' he replies, not realising the effect his bitter sarcasm has on you.

'That's not fair,' you say.

'No, it's not,' he laughs. So for the next five years you believe the ref has something to do with the other team.

You go to quite a lot of matches. Sometimes they win, sometimes they draw, and sometimes they lose. They seem to lose the most. Occasionally they score a goal and often the other team score a goal.

When the other team score, all the men around you blame the ref, the linesman, the goalie or the defenders. When your lot score they just jump up in the air and cheer, so you jump up and cheer with them. And when that happens you feel really, really, really, really, really good. You belong with the crowd. And you go to as many games as you can because of these moments - when your team scores it excuses everything else. And it's something you want to experience again and again.

You're hooked.

13

~ Coping with crap ~

1) Always expect the worst

The fact is that you are well aware your team, on the whole, are crap. But from time to time you may lose sight of this. It's a common mistake, easily made.

What happens is this…

As you languish in 18th place in the league, you find yourself watching half-decent opponents in the LDV Vans trophy. Your lot's manager has clearly told the players: 'Don't worry lads - just go out there and enjoy yourselves.'

What happens?

They play well and win. The wingers run like the wind. The strikers leap gracefully into the air before burying headers into the corner of the net. The defence plays as one, like a wall of solid rock. The goalie dives athletically to keep out anything and everything.

And the captain is commanding, a true leader, with his head held high.

The terraces are alive, the crowd's chants continue into the streets long after the game has finished.

You feel all warm inside, like you've eaten a gigantic bowl of Ready Brek. In the heat of the moment you turn to your mates and you say: 'The tide has turned. Play-offs here we come.'

They feel the same way. Everybody's smiling as they walk into the pub. Everybody's happy.

In the corner there's a wizened old man wearing a faded scarf. With a roll-up between his cracked lips he tells you not to get carried away - he's seen it all before.

Listen to the old man in the corner. He knows what he's talking about.

2) Dealing with the 90-minute ordeal

So you're there again, ready for kick-off. You're wearing the lucky underpants, you've checked to see how far up the table three points will get you (if the other results go your way), and you're trying to suppress those feelings of hope. The

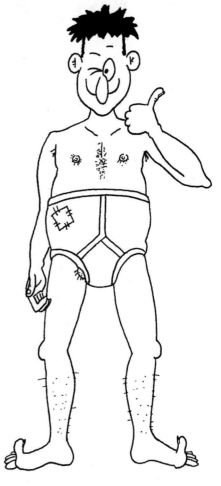

biting north wind howls mercilessly across the half-filled terraces. The rain falls out of the sky. It's minus 2 degrees...

Steel yourself, grit your teeth, pull up your
scarf and your collar, cover your ears with
your hat. The Master of Ceremonies tries to
announce the teams' line-ups but there's
something wrong with the PA system. It's par
for the course - don't worry. The amusing
animal club mascot has done a little dance,
the titchy schoolboy matchday mascots have
gone off and everyone's lined up...

The ref looks at his watch. This is usually the best point of the game - enjoy this moment. From here on in things will certainly deteriorate. But you won't be able to help nurturing some hope. It's natural. It's the reason you're there, isn't it?

OK. It's 3 o'clock. The ref has one last look around and blows his whistle.

Here we go again then…

3) Kick-off

Your team always do the same thing. It's passed back to the captain and he boots it off for a throw-in.

In 1987 you questioned this tactic but you have long since given up. There is, however, a very simple explanation. It is a superstition. The captain has not yet broken his leg, so it must be working. Don't worry about it. Just accept that your lot are not too keen on possession.

It means they have to do something.

The other team seem to have worked on kick-offs in training. They all look raring to go and when the ref blows the whistle they're off like greyhounds out of the traps. For the first 45 seconds they run rings round your lot and it's only because their striker's shot hits your goalie on the knee as he's diving the wrong way that you're not 1-0 down.

4) Corners

If your team win a corner, don't get your hopes up. They will not score from it. In the unlikely event that the ball beats the first defender, it will be headed clear by their gigantic centre back.

When he heads it clear one of two things will happen:

1 - Under the illusion that he's about to score a blindingly spectacular goal, your captain will volley the ball up and into the car park of the flats behind the south bank.

2 - One of the other team will pick it up, break away very, very fast and score, leaving your defence scattered on their arses all over the pitch.

If the other team get a corner they will score. It doesn't matter that they look almost as crap as your lot.

They appear to have been practising corners in training. It will be perfectly placed and their gigantic centre forward will rise like a gazelle and bury the ball into the corner of the net.

There's nothing you can do about it. It happens every time.

At least, it seems to.

5) Free-kicks

When your lot get a free-kick just outside
the penalty box, the other team will make a
wall, everyone else will jostle around the D,
and the captain and the right back will
stand intel-
ligently
over the
ball,
pretending
they've got
it all
worked
out. That
much is
predictable.

However,
when the
ref blows
the whistle,
one of two
things will
happen:

1 - The captain will kick the ball straight at
the wall, and one of them will then hoof it
back to your goalie.

2 - The captain will boot the ball into the car
park of the flats behind the south bank.

When the other team get a free-kick one of two things will happen:

1 - Your lot will make a wall, everyone else will jostle around the D and, when the ref blows the whistle, their captain will curl it spectacularly over the wall and into the back of the net.

2 - They will take it before anyone else is
ready.

A short pass to their striker will be followed
by him side-footing the ball into an empty
net while your goalie is still working out how
many men he wants in the wall.

6) Injuries

If one of the other team gets injured, he's faking it and playing for time. You are likely to hear a bunch of kids down the front shout 'she fell over'.

When the player does eventually get up it's customary to boo and jeer him every time he touches the ball for the rest of the match, even if he does have blood trickling down from a bandaged bonce.

If one of your lot is injured, it's genuine. If it's one of your better players he will be stretchered off and it will be something serious that will keep him sidelined for at least two months.

If it's one of your crap players he'll be OK with a quick dose of the cold, wet sponge.

7) Throw-ins

When your lot get a throw-in, the players
will stand around with their body
language saying 'don't throw it to me -
I don't want it'. It will be like watching a
game of musical statues without the music.
Eventually the ball will be chucked as far as
possible up the
line where
one of two
things will
happen:

1 - Your lot
will get
another
throw.

2 - It will fall to the
other team who will then play the ball away
with a few neat touches.
These are the only possible outcomes from
a throw-in.

When the other team get a throw-in their
players will be moving about so quickly that
your lot won't be able to keep up. They will
play the ball upfield with incisive passing
and off-the-ball movement, and get
something positive out of it.

8) Penalties

From time to time in a season the ref will blow and point at the spot. Everyone around you will cheer as if a goal has been scored, because penalties are child's play, aren't they? Well, maybe they are with other teams, but with your lot? Of course not. Never assume that a goal is inevitable.

Everyone knows, one way or another - most likely from watching it on the telly - that the best way to score from a penalty is to take a good run-up, keep the head down and smash it into the back of the net - so hard that if the goalie does happen to get anywhere near it he will simply get propelled back into the net with the ball. Yes, everyone knows that - except your lot...

When the penalty is taken the ball will:

1 - roll leisurely into the waiting arms of their keeper, or

2 - bounce three times before going the wrong side of the post.

If the penalty taker has been watching telly he will step up confidently before blasting it over the bar.

9) Half time

There will be music and dancing from the half time women, who dress like American cheerleaders and dream of one day becoming Page 3 girls. They will try to put together a few synchronised routines.

In the meantime, meat pies, hamburgers, chips and coffee are on offer to anyone willing or hungry enough to join the queue and miss the first five minutes of the second half. The coffee (or tea) will be so hot that it will melt the plastic cup.

The best way to deal with half-time cuisine is to stuff the hamburger into the coffee and then suck the burger bun throughout the second half.

The Master of Ceremonies will try to announce the half-time scores of other games. With the microphone playing up again, you will hear things like 'Man United pool one sea arse two Newcastle' interspersed with crackles and pops before things go quiet and you realise he's given up on it.

~ Players ~

Goalkeepers

Your goalie will usually be a few inches
shorter than the average goalie. However,
he's fairly dependable, but you can't deny
he gets plenty of practice during matches.

Waiting in the wings, or on the bench, you have a substitute goalie who you fear. He was signed accidentally three seasons ago and now you can't get rid of him. He's 6ft 7inches but weighs in at just under 9 stones.

Everyone knows your sub goalie is crap, and you do not want him on the pitch at any time.

Defenders

Central defenders are usually far more comfortable hitting people than tackling them. Your main central defender will be built like a brick shithouse and have a nasty scar down his left cheek.

With his thick, muscular neck, he can head the ball the full length of the pitch. He gets sent off three times every season and scores more goals than the strikers when the team's form is under par. If he makes a mistake, nobody says anything - not even the fans.

Left and right sided defenders are pretty much the same as those in Sunday league. They're merely the best of the rest, so put in defence out of the way. Left and right sided defenders are often known as utility players because they can play just as badly in any position.

When they get the ball at their feet they hoof it upfield and, although it isn't pretty to watch, you're pleased because if they try to be clever they invariably make a mess of it.

Midfielders

Central midfielders
are, more often
than not,
defenders with
a bit more
intelligence.

Your tough-
tackling
captain will
be somewhere
in here.

Occasionally he
tries to control
the ball and
sometimes he's
successful.

Having done
that, he
looks up
to see
what's on,
and then boots the ball out for a goal kick.

Wingers seem to have bags of potential which they never quite fulfil.

They can dribble fairly well when they're on form, their crossing's a bit suspect, but the main problem is that halfway through the first half they seem to run out of ideas and just sort of give up.

Wingers are blamed by the captain for not latching on to his wayward passes.

Strikers

The 6ft 3inch target man wins a lot of route one passes but, when he's done that, he looks a bit lost.

It's as if the manager's said to him 'I want you to win everything in the air' and not told him what he should do afterwards.

He doesn't appear to understand the offside rule, but still manages to score six goals every season.

The nippy little striker
is supposed to feed off the
target man but usually ends up
playing a bit deeper just so he can
have the occasional look-in.

He gets substituted in the 75th minute
looking dejected and fed-up.

Fringe players

Akin to the undead in those old Hammer Horror films, fringe players lurk about in corridors and dark rooms waiting for first team players to get injured or suspended.

They are the better reserve team players.

When they get that long-awaited call-up they run nervously out onto the pitch, blinking at the natural daylight that they haven't seen for many months. Once the game gets underway they try really hard to make some sort of impact.

They really do try. But, alas…

~ Transfers ~

Players out
While you read rumours in the tabloids of premiership teams showing interest in quality players and offering millions, it doesn't work like that in the lower leagues...

What happens is this - one day a player is in the first team and then he isn't.

No one mentions him again and it's not until you see his name in small letters in the back pages because he's scored a hat-trick that you realise he's gone elsewhere. The strange thing is that many of your transfers out seem to end up as star players at better teams than yours.

Don't ask why...

It will only end in tears.

All you really need to know is that, when he comes back with his new team, you have to boo and jeer him at every opportunity.

Players in

From time to time the local paper will report the signing of a player on a free. This news invariably comes out of the blue, and the player will be previously unheard of.

It's not unusual to read that he had a bad time at his previous club, who play in the division below your lot, but he's intent on giving everything and proving himself.

He'll be quoted saying:
'I'm very impressed with the set-up here.'

The manager will be quoted saying:
'I've had my eye on the young lad for quite some time.'

There will, understandably, be renewed hope on the terraces, and the new man will receive a welcoming and polite round of applause on his home debut. His performance will, of course, provide inspiration, and the chances are that he will put the cross in that leads to the equaliser.

In his second match he will run around for the full 90 minutes and will be slightly unlucky not to have got anything out it. The manager will praise his effort.

By the third match he will have faded away. It's as if the captain has said to him something along the lines of: 'Stop trying so hard. You're making the rest of us look bad.'

The more cynical fans will often blame this type of behaviour on the player being signed initially on a week-to-week contract. While this is ongoing he tries to impress but, once something a bit more concrete is in the bag, he takes his foot off.

But that's just the more cynical fans…

~ Supporters ~

Adult supporters can be divided into
six basic categories. These are:

The optimistic optimist

This person will, as the name implies,
always see the good side of everything. For
example, he will point out the lightning pace
of the winger, omitting the part where he
usually forgets to take the ball with him.
Having the optimistic optimist around makes
everyone nearby
feel slightly
guilty about
slagging off
the
players.

The pessimistic optimist

The pessimistic optimist is the optimistic optimist who is beginning to realise the truth of the matter.

What he thinks and what he sees on the pitch don't correlate.

He generally sits through a match without saying too much.

The coach

In his world, this character really is the team's coach.

Throughout the full 90 minutes he'll be shouting instructions as if he believes the players - who he seems to know personally - can hear him. 'Dave! Spin off!' 'Mark! Step up!' Kev! Get it down the flanks!'

He lives every kick of the match, and dreams of being in the dug-out.

The optimistic pessimist

This supporter turns up for every fifth home
match, stating that things couldn't have got
any worse than the last time.

By 3.20pm he realises they have, and by
four o'clock he's at the bus stop.

The pessimistic pessimist

The pessimistic pessimist goes
to every match and hates
every moment of it. He sits
on an aisle seat with one
leg outstretched, arms
tightly crossed and
an expression
of anger etched
into his
features.

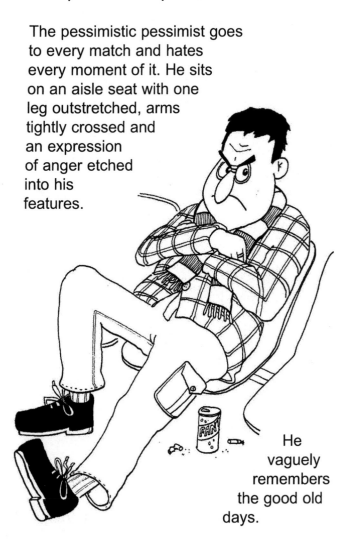

He
vaguely
remembers
the good old
days.

The thug

He goes to matches for the tribal element.

He'll be there with his mates, singing songs, trying to get a laugh with his one-liners, and hoping for some sort of trouble.

Contrary to media opinion, he is there primarily for the football and loves his team unconditionally.

The thug goes to away matches.

~ Away matches ~

Travel to away matches is not recommended. If you can stay up late enough, it is possible to watch your lot's highlights on the telly and, if they happen to score, there is a small cheer from the 38 hardy souls who have braved the 600-mile round trip.

You talk in hushed tones of one day joining them.

That's understandable, but let's look at what they do, exactly...

While self-proclaimed supporters of top premiership teams are fairly unlikely to actually live in that team's city, your lot will not have any home fans who travel any further than from Acacia Avenue, over on the posh side of town.

There are, of course, the ex-pats dotted in various places around the country and in Australia, Canada and New Zealand, who have ways of finding out the result on a Saturday afternoon.

If the match is on a Tuesday or Wednesday night, the first thing you must do is book the day off work or throw a sickie.

You must allow for rush-hour mayhem, so leave home accordingly. Let's say you leave at 2pm. You travel with a certain amount of pre-match optimism - this is dangerous. Although you are on the road, away from your usual environs, you must try to keep a grip on reality. Just because you are making the effort, it doesn't mean your players are going to.

The rain starts falling at 2.30pm and by 6pm, when you're eating saveloy and chips in a greasy chip shop, it will turn to snow.

We now move forward to 8.30pm. It's half time, you're 3-0 down, cold, miserable, 300 miles from home, being mocked by the home fans, and wondering why you bothered.

Well, don't say we didn't tell you so…

~ Everyday life ~

In your life outside of the stadium, it is likely that you will talk about football with others.

The majority of these will support premiership teams like Manchester United, Liverpool and Arsenal. They will support them only in that they look out for their results and say 'yes' when they win, or that they watch matches on the telly.

When you talk about your team the other person will smile. He will be mildly amused by your blind faith in what he considers to be the crap local team.

There are two things you need to know:

1 - He's right.

2 - There's nothing you can do to change his opinion. From time to time you may successfully persuade someone to go with you to a match. Your lot will repay you by playing worse than ever.

You will never win over someone who is used to watching ten minutes of premiership highlights while sprawled across a comfy sofa with a mug of cocoa on the arm.

It doesn't compare to 90 minutes of hopeless endeavour in freezing temperatures.

As you traipse disconsolately homewards after yet another crap match you will probably turn to your fellows and say, gloomily: 'Never again.'

It'll probably make you feel a little better for a few seconds, but really you're just wasting your breath.

You don't need to be told that you're kidding yourself.

The fact is that you know you support a
crap football team.

But deep down, you're still proud of them.